*Peace*
*Flows*
*from*
*the*
*Sky*

Other books by

# Blue Mountain Press INC.

**Come Into the Mountains, Dear Friend**
by Susan Polis Schutz
**I Want to Laugh, I Want to Cry**
by Susan Polis Schutz
**Someone Else to Love**
by Susan Polis Schutz
**I'm Not That Kind of Girl**
by Susan Polis Schutz
**Yours If You Ask**
by Susan Polis Schutz

**The Best Is Yet to Be**
**Step to the Music You Hear, Vol. I**
**The Language of Friendship**
**The Language of Love**
**The Language of Happiness**
**The Desiderata of Happiness**
by Max Ehrmann
**Whatever Is, Is Best**
by Ella Wheeler Wilcox
**Poor Richard's Quotations**
by Benjamin Franklin
**I Care About Your Happiness**
by Kahlil Gibran/Mary Haskell
**My Life and Love Are One**
by Vincent Van Gogh
**I Wish You Good Spaces**
by Gordon Lightfoot
**We Are All Children Searching for Love**
by Leonard Nimoy
**Catch Me with Your Smile**
by Peter McWilliams
**Creeds to Love and Live By**

# *Peace Flows from the Sky*

By
Susan Polis Schutz

Designed and illustrated by
Stephen Schutz

**Blue Mountain Press** ™.

Boulder, Colorado

Library of Congress Number: 74-26027
ISBN: 0-88396-007-9

Manufactured in the United States of America

The following poem has appeared earlier:
"When a person has a real friend," Copyright © Continental
Publications, 1973.

First Printing: November, 1974
Second Printing: February, 1975
Third Printing: January, 1976
Fourth Printing: November, 1976
Fifth Printing: May, 1978

**Blue Mountain Press** INC.

P.O. Box 4549, Boulder, Colorado 80306

# CONTENTS

# INTRODUCTION

I am lucky because I can share my life through my poetry. Each of my books reflects changes I have gone through, as well as observations I have made during the time they were written.

*Peace Flows from the Sky* finds me living with the man I love in a home surrounded on all sides by the beautiful Rocky Mountains. I've had time to get to know nature, to appreciate the perfect relationship I have with Stephen, and to think about many other things that are important to me.

Again, thank you for listening.

S.P.S.
November, 1974

# I

Peace flows
from the sky
through the air
to me.

The fluffy pearl clouds
move from one pine tree
to another
high above the rocky mountains.

The birds' singing
brings me out of my trance
to remind me of life
and who I am.

I am a
very tiny,
tiny
part of the world...
a part that
is lucky enough
to be able to
touch the beauty
of nature.

The crickets
sing
and the ants
dance.
The marmots
sing
and the rocks
dance.
The birds
sing
and the leaves
dance.

And I sit
in the grass
so lucky
to hear this
magnificent
symphony.

Alone
we are
two separate
individuals
trying to survive
Together
we are
strength
and
truth
and
nature
in a world
of love

Colorado
where the mountains reign
and the dry clear air
makes one always want to
be outside

Colorado
a place to be whoever you want
there is no style to follow
no symbols needed to prove yourself

Colorado
land of horses
and cows
and people
just happy to be alive

Colorado
land of the sun
mountain of peace

A house
is a place where one lives,
as is a
basement.
But this house
is special.
High in the sky,
our house sits
on a large mountain
looking out on the
whole city.
Lights blink below
like a year round Christmas.
From the deck,
we inhale
the pine tree air
while watching
the twinkling magic.
Our neighbors,
the deer, cactus and birds,
create a very
peaceful family.
Sitting in our windowy
living room,
we are on
top of the world
and so far away
from things.
A house
is a place
where one lives.
But our house
is a place where one loves.

When you are not with me
my life is so different
I barely function in my daily tasks
and do just what is expected of me
and no more

When you are near me
I am a complete person
involved in all my work
I am a burst of life
looking forward to
each new second

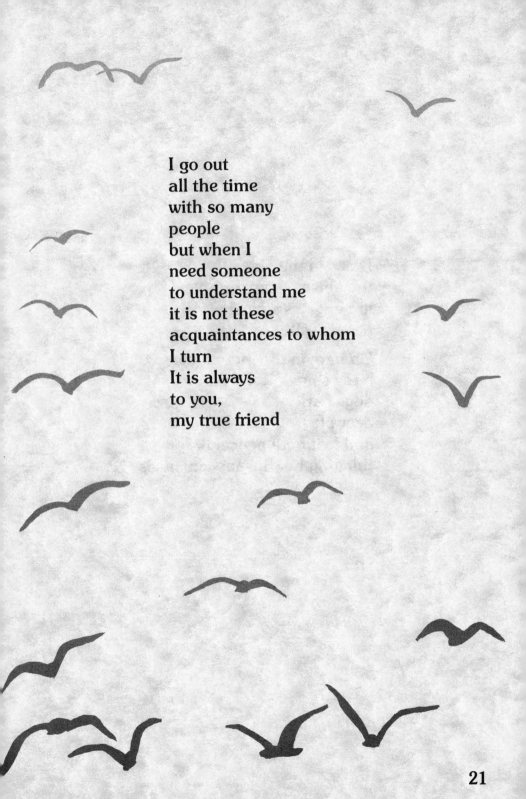

I go out
all the time
with so many
people
but when I
need someone
to understand me
it is not these
acquaintances to whom
I turn
It is always
to you,
my true friend

Down in the city
the noise of cars rumble
fire engines squeal
people yell

Up here in the mountains
birds sing
dogs bark
deer play
and I sit here peacefully
thinking how insane city life is

I left the mountains
for a trip to the city
Oh — the lights
the restaurants
the theaters
the people
the action

It was fun
but not nearly as much fun
as coming home
to the mountains

When a person has a real friend, he learns not only to appreciate another human being, but he also learns to understand himself better.

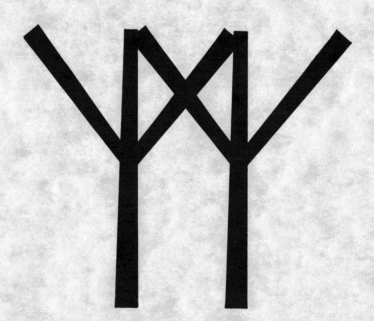

Ancient Friendship Symbol

I haven't seen you in a while
yet I often imagine
all your expressions

I haven't spoken to you recently
but many times
I hear your thoughts

Good friends must not always
be together
It is the feeling of oneness
when distant
that proves a lasting friendship

If you have a goal in life
that takes a lot of energy
that requires a lot of work
that incurs a great deal of interest
and that is a challenge to you

You will always look
forward to waking up
to see what the new day brings

If you have a person in your life
that understands you completely
that shares your ideas
that trusts you
and believes in everything you do

You will always look
forward to the night
because you will never be lonely

I am so proud
as you walk so straight down the road
stopping to pat little children's heads

I am so proud
when you hike in the woods
and feed stray animals

I am so proud
when you look at me so softly
and the whole world can
see your feelings

I am so proud
to exchange myself with you
and for us to become one

Though we
drifted apart in distance
I always
think of you as being right here
Though we have different interests
our experiences are still the same
and though we
have many new friends
it is our old and
continuous friendship
that means the most to me

There is no need
for an outpouring of
words to explain oneself
to a friend.
Friends understand each
other's thoughts even before
they are spoken.

When someone cares
it is easier to speak
it is easier to listen
it is easier to play
it is easier to work

When someone cares
it is easier to laugh

I want to wake him
and say thank you
thank you for
knowing me

I want to wake him
and say thank you
thank you for
understanding me

I want to wake him
and say thank you
thank you for
making me so happy

I want to wake him
and say thank you
thank you for transforming me
into erotic delirium

But there he sleeps
so quiet and peaceful
I'll just kiss him softly
and thank him tomorrow

Sometimes
when I am
sitting alone
I think of you
Sometimes
when I am
out with a lot
of people
I think of you
Always when I
want to talk to
someone
I think of you

# II

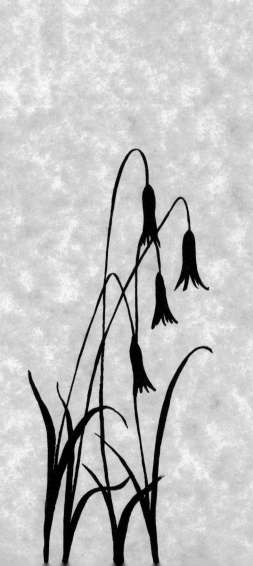

Many women I know
told me that
they never felt
complete
until they had
their first
baby
I don't understand
this
Why can't women
feel complete
in themselves
like men
do

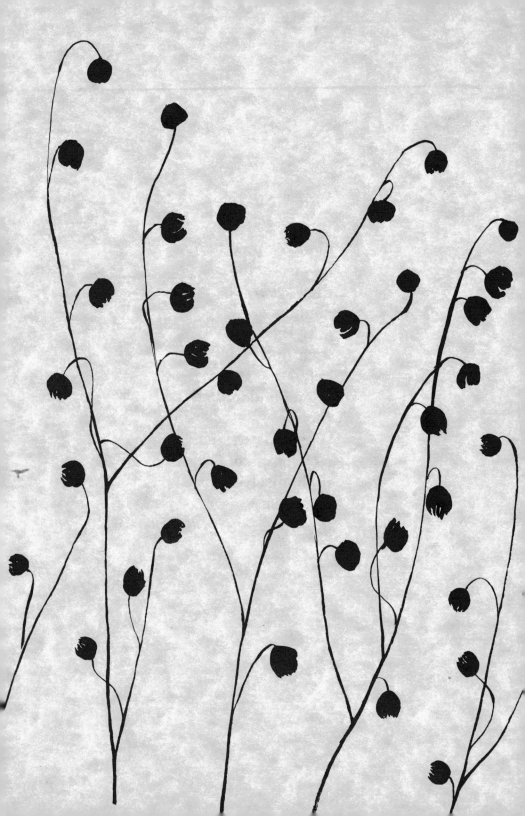

Everyone wants to know
where poets write.
They picture the poet
sitting in front of a fire
in a rustic log cabin,
or perhaps in front of
a beautiful oak roll-top desk
in a large room with stained glass
windows.

If I told you I write
on the beach
and in the mountains,
you would like me.

If I told you I write
under the hair dryer,
in the shower
and in bed,
you would dislike me,
because I'm destroying
the glamorous myth of poets.

The truth is,
a poet writes
everywhere,
anywhere or
anytime she is inspired.

Should I have
a child
now?
It would probably
be so cute,
and it could
live in the
empty room
near ours.
But should I
have a child
now?
It might
mean months of
nausea
and interference
with my
career and
life.
It will
mean
some pain,
(which I hate),
and then a lifetime
of sharing another
person with us.

When you are a struggling
straggling young artist
people love you

When you can not afford breakfast
and live in a dirty basement
people say what a dedicated artist you are

When you spend your time creating
and have no time left for friends
people say that you are a true artist

When you sell your first creation
everyone cheers
When you sell your second creation
everyone is happy

But, as your creations gain recognition
and your name is known
many of these same people hate you

Fame grows and there is a real
demand for your work
Some people say you are now commercial

And many of the same people say
"an overnight success," "doesn't deserve it,"
"creates for the public,"
"not a true artist at all"

They forget the years of struggle
They forget that a person does not
change his creations just because he
is successful
They forget that this is one of the
things for which every artist strives

Why can't these same people
share your happiness as
they shared your struggle?

When love is beautiful
the poem about love
should be beautiful
but if it is
there are those people
who call it "light and soppy"

When the sky is clear blue
and the mountain air crisp
the poem about nature
should be beautiful
but if it is
there are those people
who call it "light and soppy"

When the birds sing
and the flowers bloom
the poem about life
should be beautiful
but if it is
there are those people
who call it "light and soppy"

But when
love is unrequited
and suicide contemplated
these same people
call the poem a work of art

Something is very wrong
when people are so
ashamed of beautiful feelings
that they call them "light and soppy"
while being so proud of anguish
that they equate it
with being an intellectual

Something is very sad
about people who feel this way
(or at least say they do)
They will never be
free from themselves
to experience any kind
of beauty in their lives

I saw a famous
publisher enter his
hotel room with
his arm around a
young girl,
his devoted wife
at home.
I always held
this man in
very high esteem,
but now I could
never again do
business with him.
If he could do this
to the woman he loves,
what would he do
to a business associate
that he likes?

New York City is the
most interesting place to live
Millions of people
bumping into you
each with an interesting story to share
A world center for
industry, publishers,
stock market, museums,
concerts, plays, television,
and most
everything else

There is always
something new to discover
or someone new to meet
One's mind is always challenged
New York City is an international city
A world of its own

If you could take the Colorado outdoors
and put it in New York City
then you'd have a perfect city
But since you can't
New York City remains a place for your mind
but not for your soul

I am a woman
thrilled to be part of an exciting career
happy to converse with all types of people
ecstatic to be involved in a perfect love
free to say whatever I feel
lucky to share a real family
content to sit in the mountains and just think

I am a person
proud to be a
woman
I am a woman
proud to be
alive

How could you have the
nerve to say
"No woman of mine will have a career"
Do you realize what you are saying
You are saying that you are superior
You can have a career
but your woman must sit quietly at home
You are saying that you can be around people
but your woman must speak only to children
You are saying that you can be stimulated by events
but your woman must be stimulated from washing
     the floor
You are saying that if
your woman has a career
you would no longer be the total center
of everything your woman does
You are saying that your woman
must deteriorate
(you know that is what will happen if
you don't let her use her mind)
You are saying
that your woman must have no goals of her own
that your woman must have no ideas of her own
that your woman must have no life of her own

You are a murderer

Music transcends all barriers
among people
Slow soft songs
　　eyes are sad and misty
Fast songs
　　eyes are sparkling
Old familiar songs
　　eyes are dreamy
Witty songs
　　eyes are laughing

No matter who we are
or where we come from
when listening to music
we are all one

Please, people,
listen to him.
He is
making
music.
He is
trying to
entertain you.
He is
showing you
his soul.
Please, people,
listen to him.

If you want to live in the country
If you want to live in the city
If you want to be a carpenter
If you want to be an artist

Do it!

If you want to tell someone they are right
If you want to tell someone they are wrong
If you want to tell someone you are happy
If you want to tell someone you are sorry

Tell it!

Do you like to dress neat?
Do you like to dress sloppy?
Do you want to have long hair?
Do you want to have short hair?

> Look it.

Do you want to love men?
Do you want to love women?
Do you want a lot of friends?
Do you want to be alone?

> Do it.

If you feel like screaming
If you feel like laughing
If you feel like talking
If you feel like being silent

> Feel it.

Do it.
Tell it.
Look it.
Feel it.
Now.
It's your only chance.
Live the life you dream.
Dream the life you live.

What is it
in a woman
that causes her
to be so full of life
ideas and excitement
when young
but right after marriage
to lose all interests
and all capabilities
outside of
keeping house and
seeing that her
husband is fit

Is it the fault
of the husbands
whose careers and
egos must be nurtured
to the point where the
woman has
no energy left for
herself

Or is it the fault
of society
which trains the woman
that the most important
thing she can do
is to get a successful man
and that the woman
needn't develop
her own mind and
activities once this
goal is reached

Or is it the fault
of the woman
who sees
the world outside
and what it has
done to her father
and her husband
and she takes
the easy way out
by not joining the world

Though each woman
has a different
reason for her decay
we all need to
overcome the reason and
overcome the cause and
immediately seek
an interesting
life of our own

Well dear mate
Why are you so late
Whom did you talk to
What did you do
Were you alone
So many hours away from me
I'm lonely, can't you see

Please dear beau
Let me know
With whom did you speak
With whom did you meet
With whom did you dine
What papers did you sign
So many hours away from me
I'm lonely, can't you see

Our relationship
is so strong
because we
treat each other
as equals in
every aspect of
life
and because
we are completely
truthful with
each other
in every word and
thought

Why do I write?
I write because
I see something
or touch something
or smell something
or feel something
that I can not understand
until I try to describe it
in written
words.

My favorite place to write
is right here
surrounded by the tall mountains
above which is the dark blue Colorado sky
Here I lie
so content to be
At this time
I could not write
a bad word
or a derogatory sentence
because that's just not
the way the mountains
inspire me

I honestly believe that if
everyone only had the chance to
lie here quietly
admiring the scenery
there would be no more
destruction
because this kind of
peace envelops
our entire being
If only everyone had
this chance

## ABOUT THE AUTHORS

Susan and Stephen are the best-selling poet-artist team in the United States. Their first six books, Come Into the Mountains, Dear Friend; I Want to Laugh, I Want to Cry; Peace Flows from the Sky; Someone Else to Love; I'm Not That Kind of Girl; and Yours If You Ask, are continual best-sellers, with combined sales of well over one million copies. In addition, their poetry and illustrations have appeared on over 50 million notecards and prints, and have drawn exceptional response from numerous readers.

After attending graduate school, Susan worked as a teacher, a social worker and a newspaper reporter. In addition to writing six poetry books and editing a variety of others, she has had many articles published in magazines and newspapers and is working on an autobiographical novel.

Stephen studied at the New York High School of Music and Art, the Boston Museum of Fine Arts School, the Massachusetts Institute of Technology, and received a Ph.D. from Princeton University in 1970. Stephen, who has designed and illustrated all of Susan's books, is well known for his original calligraphy, serigraph techniques and airbrush paintings.